# GEN NOW

LANCE J. RICHARDS
JASON S. MORGA

# ABOUT THE AUTHORS

**LANCE J. RICHARDS, GPHR, SPHR, HRMP** is Vice President, Innovation for Kelly Services. Previously, he headed KellyOCG's Human Resources Consulting practice, where he had overall accountability for the practice on a global basis. Lance is a frequent writer and speaker, providing thought leadership on workforce strategy and evolution. Lance has over 20 years of executive roles in cross-border HR.

**Linkedin:** Linkedin.com/in/lancejrichards
**Twitter:** @lancejrichards
**Email:** Lance.richards@kellyservices.com

**JASON S. MORGA, PHR** is Vice President, Americas Marketing for Kelly Services. His group delivers a wide range of interactive and media-rich solutions to support internal and external Kelly clients. Jason is also an Innovation Champion for Kelly's Office of Innovation and has been engaged in human resources and marketing for more than 15 years.

**Linkedin:** Linkedin.com/in/jasonmorga
**Twitter:** @jasonsmorga
**Email:** Jason.morga@kellyservices.com

## Acknowledgements

We worked diligently on this book, but we also borrowed bandwidth and time from family, friends and co-workers… hoping to get this thing right. We gratefully acknowledge the following folks who all helped us bring this book to life:

Lori Beirne-Kennedy
Grete and Cameron Carder
Kimberly Coticchia
Dominique Hanlon
Josie Huber
Michael Kirsten
Jocelyn Lincoln
Melissa McAward
Vonda, Brynlie and Kylie Morga
Megan Raftery
Franchette and Brianna Richards
Leslie and Colin Sheidler
Justine Webse
Mona Wehbe

Kelly Services
999 W Big Beaver Rd
Troy MI 48084
USA

# Contents

# Welcome to the successful organization of tomorrow

Here, four generations of skilled, knowledgeable workers collaborate to realize a shared vision that drives ground-breaking innovation and productivity.

This workforce aims to accumulate results, rather than hours at a desk. To this end, it comprises experts of all ages who work from home, a hotel, the airport lounge or anywhere else they can leverage technology to perform meaningful, engaging work that really makes a difference. The word 'office' has truly morphed from a place to something one does… from noun to verb.

It allows them the freedom to live *then* work, not the other way around. They're an upbeat, eclectic bunch, with bonds forged via instant messaging and social media, and, of course, a shared passion for their work.

Change is exciting in this place. It is embraced, sought out, not avoided. Education is ingrained in the culture, but not in the traditional sense or structures. Here, everyone learns. And everyone teaches.

Here, talent stays. Office costs are comparatively low, given the flexible just-in-time work model employed. These savings, along with sustained profitability, make for a healthy bottom line, which in turn makes room for investment. This organization's brand just keeps evolving and its followers multiply.

The phenomenon known as 'the skills gap' is something only the outliers who haven't *quite* made the transition to the new world of work will experience.

Sound like a corporate vision of Utopia, where *Brave New World* meets *The Office*? Brace yourself—because it might not be as farfetched, or as far off, as you think.

# A redefined workforce needs a redefined workplace—like yesterday!

You've already read plenty about the challenges presented by the multi-generational workforce. You get it. The generations are wired differently, they work differently and organizations have to adapt or they'll go the way of the dinosaur.

So, you've been working on your adaptation strategies ... how's that working out so far? Have you started to see progress within your organization? How about within your department?

The brutal truth is that you don't have much time to change. Improving productivity, reducing turnover and building your talent supply chain across four diverse age groups—and beyond—is imperative for organizational success as we stare down the barrel of a changing workplace.

When preparing this publication, we were mindful of how much has already been covered regarding generational issues in the workplace —in particular, in 'dealing with' Gen Y. It's the reason we reviewed more than 50 papers, studies and surveys—from those of leading think tanks to ones published by the Big Four consulting firms. We absorbed an enormous volume of articles in various periodicals—from *The Economist,* to a one-paragraph blurb from patch.com. And we made good use of the

2012 and 2013 *Kelly Global Workforce Index*, an annual primary research exercise, which comprised information from 122,000 respondents across 31 countries. In 2012 alone it included over 46,000 Gen Ys. Specifically, in 2013:

**Gen X**
35%

**Gen Y**
46%

**Baby Boomers**
18%

From all of this research, we can tell you that there are fundamental reasons why organizations, not just HR departments and HR leaders, must respond to generational issues —and quickly.

And, most importantly, we can suggest strategies that will also assist in creating a workplace that grapples much less with recruiting, engaging and retaining top talent — even in the face of the aging and declining workforce, and the prospect of a dysfunctional multi-gen workforce.

The fact is, although there is a deluge of anecdotal evidence suggesting that the different generations' mindsets and approaches to work are worlds apart, we now know that the modern workplace is occupied by a constituency that—across the age spectrum:

- demands flexible conditions and work/life balance,

- thrives on collaboration and entrepreneurialism, and

- at once craves knowledge/is qualified to impart it.

Today's workforce needs to believe in its employer and perceive meaning in its work, too.

Where once we may have been daunted by the prospect of the much-maligned and little-understood Gen Y, or the Millennial generation, representing over 45% of the workforce, our research indicates that this demographic brings a fresh approach to the table. In combination with the experience and knowledge of the generations before them, this could be the exact solution business needs.

The simple truth? If leaders can adapt their mindsets and processes to embrace genuine integration of the learning and leadership styles of Baby Boomers, Gen Xs and Gen Ys, they will bolster their success—and resilience—in the changing world of work.

# A new workplace, a new workforce

There are a number of social and economic factors that have culminated to define the modern workplace and the workforce that embodies it.

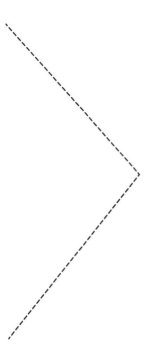

The accelerating pace of technological advancement, for example, means that there is great pressure for organizations not simply to keep up but to stay ahead of the game. Everything, from the methods and media through which we communicate, to the products and services with which we strive to remain competitive, is subject to constant innovation. The pressure to deliver, and often deliver *yesterday*, sees a large proportion of workers engaging in work for much longer than their allotted 40 hours per week. According to *Forbes*:

*To get ahead, a 70-hour work week is the new standard ... 1.7 million people consider their jobs and their work hours extreme, thanks to*

*globalization, BlackBerries [sic], corporate expectations and their own*
*Type A personalities.*[1]

The modern workplace is also defined by the looming skills shortage, caused in part by an aging and declining workforce, which is a global phenomenon taking place in all industries and across traditional boundaries. Workers aged 55 years and older are expected to comprise 24 percent of the workforce by 2018, compared to 31 percent in 2013. More than 78 million Baby Boomers are being followed by a far smaller cohort of 45 million Gen X workers, so there will be a shrinking pool of prime-aged workers to fill the gaps. The demand for talented Gen X leaders will increase, but the supply will decrease.

As well, people are remaining in the workforce longer than they used to and not just because their pension plans took a beating in the global financial crisis. Besides financial pressures, the prospect of post-work boredom is chief among the reasons that people delay retirement, or opt for flexible or temporary work past retirement age.

In fact, these delayed retirements could manifest themselves in a 'retirement bubble'. What happens when all those older workers who've delayed their retirement for financial reasons are suddenly able to leave the workforce? Ah, that's a topic for a different paper... but it bears thinking about...

The skills shortage is also attributable to organizations' inability to retain top talent. Worldwide, 43 percent of workers are considering

---

1    http://www.nbcnews.com/id/17030672/ns/business-forbescom/

quitting their jobs.[2] Gen Xs are frustrated due to lack of opportunity for advancement[3], and even though their dissipation from the workforce has slowed, highly experienced and knowledgeable Baby Boomers are still slipping through organizations' fingers. In short, there will still be a significant deficit in leadership and the competition for older, more experienced leaders.

And then there is the arrival (with a resounding thud!) of Gen Y, who by 2025 will constitute a whopping 75 percent of the global workforce.[4] Not only are traditional corporate structures out of step with the way Gen Ys want to work, but the recession has forced Millennials to walk the paths of non-traditional employment[5] and education. This has forever altered the group's perception of what 'work' is and, unsurprisingly, preventing them from being able to just 'fall in' with the career status quo. In Australia alone, this generation has an annual job turnover rate of 40 percent, with two-thirds of Gen Y workers up and leaving each job they hold within two years.[6]

We will find that we'll be placing Gen Ys into leadership roles far, far earlier in their lives than prior generations. Do we have training and development functions ready to accommodate this demand?

---

2   *2013 Kelly Global Workforce Index* Key Insights presentation
3   http://www.evolvedemployer.com/2012/01/18/why-companies-cant-ignore-gen-x/
4   http://www.forbes.com/sites/85broads/2012/01/23/gen-y-workforce-and-workplace-are-out-of-sync/
5   http://www.forbes.com/sites/85broads/2012/01/23/gen-y-workforce-and-workplace-are-out-of-sync/
6   http://www.myrecruitonline.com/events-news/MyRecruitOnline_Gen_Y.html

Suffice to say, Gen Y is not prepared to settle for less when it comes to work. And organizations, with their dwindling supplies of skilled talent, are feeling the sting of rejection.

## One work place, multiple generations

So how should businesses juggle their responses to what are, ostensibly, the symptoms of a tumultuous world? HR and work commentators the world over have made the point that it simply isn't enough for organizations to just pay lip service to the large-scale changes that are in play.

A multi-generational workforce requires trans-generational solutions: the diversity of experience and knowledge offered by four distinct generational mindsets can provide tangible benefits if leveraged and managed well.

The challenge for employers is to embrace the talent mix, tap into it, and use its strengths to deliver operational performance.

Before we launch into hard-and-fast definitions of the different generations, we want to point out that there are many ways to define them, and clearly, not all are correct for every member of a single generation. We also recognize that even the age ranges vary considerably, depending on the source used. However, the following explanations summarize the 'generational glue'—or common experiences—that define their world view and hold them together.

## THE SILENT GENERATION—THE TRADITIONALISTS

The Silent Generation is the segment of the population born between 1925 and 1945. The label was coined in a 1951 *Time* article about young people coming of age, who were born during the Great Depression and World War II. Almost two-thirds are married and 29 percent are widowed or divorced. Three-quarters are grandparents and 26 percent have a post-graduate degree. The technologies this generation developed included radio, movies, radar and instant cameras – innovations that laid the groundwork for many technological advances in the late 20th century.

Traditionalists are usually the parents of Baby Boomers. They value hard work, dedication, respect for authority, conformity and adherence to rules. The work ethic of the Silent Generation was built around responsibility and long-term commitment, so they usually prefer the status quo and can be slow to embrace change. This generation of workers shared common experiences of hardship, war and socioeconomic conflicts. Some even remember living through the Great Depression as children.

For most of them, the experiences they shared and the challenges they faced brought a sense of camaraderie that subsequent generations have never experienced in quite the same way.

It should be noted too that this Generation now comprises a very small proportion of the workforce. In the U.S. this is somewhere in the order of three percent and declining daily, so even though we do refer to the opinions of this generation throughout our work, we acknowledge that their small numbers often make statistical analysis of their collective views rather limited. Our own research does collect views of Silent Gen workers, but we acknowledge the statistical limitations.

## BABY BOOMERS—THE 'ME' GENERATION

Baby Boomers were born following World War II, between 1946 and 1964—a time that was marked by a 'booming' increase in birth rates.

Baby Boomers are generally associated with rejecting or redefining traditional values in favor of personal gratification. Most are married, many have been married more than once and one-third is now grandparents. Seventy-seven percent of all Baby Boomers are employed and two-thirds work full-time. They are a highly educated group, with 39 percent having earned a post-high school degree. Technological advances that these workers can take credit for include the microwave, VCRs, hand-held calculators, computers, color televisions, and credit cards. Many Baby Boomers have delayed their retirement; 80 percent will continue to work as contractors or free agents part-time or part of the year. In a sense, this generation has redefined 'retirement'… it's no longer a cliff-like event, but rather a gradual shift.

Having grown up in a time of affluence, Baby Boomers are optimistic and genuinely expect society to improve over time. Their developmental years were marked by many turbulent times including the Cold War, the civil rights movement, women's liberation, and political assassinations.

A common bond that they came to depend upon was the emergence of music as a regular part of life and society.

Pursuit of personal growth is a key goal of Baby Boomers, who are often called the 'me' or 'ageless' generation. They are independent, over-achieving multi-taskers who work long hours and struggle with balancing their life and work. Statistics show that they really care about the future of their companies, and they are loyal, strong performers. Kelly Services® data shows that Baby Boomers who work as free agents or temporary contractors on assignment have a higher retention rate than their younger cohorts. They typically work 22 percent more hours than workers from other generations, average 3.32 years tenure with employers, and receive 94 percent positive feedback ratings
from customers.

## GEN X—THE BRIDGE GENERATION

Gen X is the generation born after the end of the baby boom. Sometimes called the 'Baby Busters,' demographers usually define this group as people born between the mid-1960s and 1981.They are small
in number compared to the generations before and after them. This means that we have insufficient Gen X to cover our leadership demands over the coming years... hence the requirement that we get Gen Y up to speed quickly!

Nearly two-thirds of this generation comprises parents, one-third is made up of working parents, and the divorce rate among Gen X workers is nearly 50 percent (yikes!). This is the best educated generation in the workforce today, with more than 40 percent having earned a college degree or higher. They tend to reject authority and embrace risk, and are willing to jump from job to job to pursue growth and opportunity. Gen X workers are self-reliant, techno-literate, global thinkers—and they place a high value on working to live, rather than living to work.

Considered a 'bridge' generation, Gen X workers typically demand short-term payoffs with immediate feedback and rewards for a job well done. They are interested in climbing the corporate ladder, but can be cynical and frustrated by tradition. They often question hierarchy, formal authority, and traditional institutions, preferring to have more control over their time and their future. They are the first to blur the lines between the workplace and home, and they have brought about workplace changes such as telecommuting and on-site child care. Gen X does not value the same things Baby Boomers considered to be important, so employers should not expect management styles used for Baby Boomers to work well with Gen X.

The developmental years of Gen X were marked by economic stagnation, with serious societal developments such as the AIDS crisis, increasing poverty, rising divorce rates, and moms going back to work. Gen X workers grew up with MTV and cable television, and are intimately familiar with technological innovations such as floppy disks, personal computers, cell phones, DVD, and e-mail. For Gen Xs, computers have always been a part of their lives. But because PC networks and the Internet didn't exist in their early years, this group became technically apt and comfortable working independently. Although group interactions in person decreased, computers and cell phones still made it possible for Gen Xs to collaborate—only in different ways than ever before.

## GEN Y—THE MILLENNIALS

Gen Y, also dubbed Generation Next or Echo Boomers, is now entering the workforce at a rapid pace, and there are about 70 million of them. Many demographers suggest that this generation was born between 1982 and the turn of the millennium. Nearly one-third is currently attending a college or university, and their parents, family, religion, and generosity are of central importance. They display a high tolerance toward other cultures and lifestyles, and they volunteer in their communities more than prior generations did. Gen Ys join organizations and causes not because they have to, but because they want to—because they want to contribute to something significant. They are moral and committed, and they value personal achievement.

Often called the Millennials, Gen Y workers are definitely a different breed. Ambitious and demanding, they question everything and need constant feedback at work because they get it in every other aspect of their lives. If they don't see a good reason for working late or making a long commute, they usually won't do it. Loyalty to one company is not their strong suit, although they are generally very loyal to their profession and the people they work with. In a recent survey of Millennials, nearly all of the respondents (92 percent!) said that having 'meaning' in their work was of utmost importance. But when asked if they were actually getting meaning out of their work, only about a quarter of them said they were. So there is an enormous disconnection here.

Gen Y is the largest consumer group in history. Although they grew up in a time of economic prosperity, Gen Y workers have experienced life-defining events such as school violence and terrorism. The technological expertise of these hipsters has been influenced by the rapid growth of the Internet, iPods®, smart phones, text messaging, high-definition TV, and Xbox®/PlayStation® gaming. Their world is smaller than that of any other generation, thanks to technology that has brought the world to them. 'Global' means something entirely different to Gen Y than it did to previous generations. They use iPhones® to talk to people on the other side of the planet, instantaneously. They communicate with each other via e-mail, Skype™, Facebook™, and Twitter™.

## TOMORROW'S GENERATION

As Figure 1 shows, Gen Y alone represented almost 40 percent of the United States labor force by 2012. In aggregate, Gen X and Gen Y represented 70 percent of the workforce by the same year.

And there's another generation waiting in the wings to make its debut.

FIGURE 1. The four generations in today's workforce

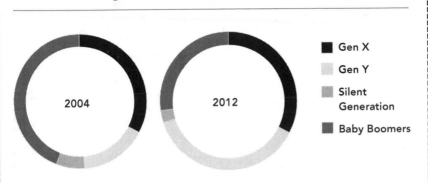

Source: Bureau of Labor Statistics

FIGURE 2. The aging workforce

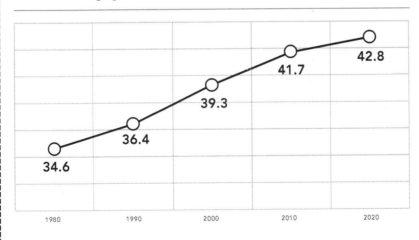

## GEN Z – THE INTERNET GENERATION

First, full disclosure: Both of your authors are raising Gen Z kids. We're living this, watching this, and wrestling with it every night at bedtime.

The next generation to hit the labor force will be the most technology-enabled generation yet. Gen Z were holding Gameboys® and Leapsters® in their hands at a very early age.

The latest Gen Zs have an iPod Touch velcroed to their crib, with apps that are built for two-to-six-month-olds... seeking to develop visual acuity, before they can even unclench their tiny fists.

They are used to seeing computers in the kitchen; Wi-Fi signals are ubiquitous. Every classroom they have been in has had a PC; and they probably started carrying a cell phone by the time they were 12 years old. They have watched their Gen X parents juggling cell phones and smart phones, and they are intimately familiar with texting and instant messaging. Many are likely to spend more time communicating electronically with their parents than sitting at the dinner table talking to them.

As the workforce continues to age and decline, whether we like it or not, this new generation will turn the supply and demand equation upside down—they will own their employers, and they will make unprecedented demands on the workplace.

And, irony of ironies, the Millennials will have to manage them.

Long-term survival and ongoing resilience of the modern workplace is not subject only to the deft management of a multi-generational workforce, but also it requires that new approaches to productivity are developed to counter the aging and declining workforce. The current practice of working longer and harder is unsustainable for many reasons, but its detrimental effect on employee wellbeing and, ultimately, the bottom line will certainly have the greatest impact on the overall health of an organization. And we have at least one generation of workers – now the dominant one – who reject this practice.

What are leaders to do?

In his recent *FastCompany* series, Robert Safian introduced Generation Flux, the group of workers who thrive in the frenetic environment that is the bi-product of an era where the 'dizzying velocity of change in our economy has made chaos the defining feature of modern business'. Safian says that 'GenFlux' workers can be any age; it is their state of mind that confirms their inclusion:

*an embrace of adaptability and flexibility; an openness to learning from anywhere; decisiveness tempered by the knowledge that business life today can shift radically every three months or so …* [7]

Our research certainly supports Safian's position that there is a generation of workers who embrace this frenetic modern workplace, regardless of their age.[8] And even if your organization contains workers who *don't* thrive in such a space, but in fact suffer through a perpetual state of

---

7   http://www.fastcompany.com/3001734/secrets-generation-flux
8   *2013 KGWI Key Insights*

overwhelmed overwork, surely introducing approaches and strategies that ease their plight and increase their effectiveness will provide relief for the worker, his or her manager and the organization itself.

Even with the identification of ageless Generation Flux, there is no going past the fact that in many ways (and unsurprisingly) it is Gen Y that embodies the cultural, economic and industrial mindset of the current epoch. Workplace trends such as continuous feedback, flexible work arrangements, work/life balance, innovation and a focus on technology are at the very heart of Gen Y attitudes. This group is the future of the world's labor force, so it is only logical that organizations should be trying to get with the Millennial program—yet if we consider that embracing 'the Gen Y way' actually stands to benefit the multi-gen workforce and boost productivity, then the mission has just increased in urgency!

## Scenario 1

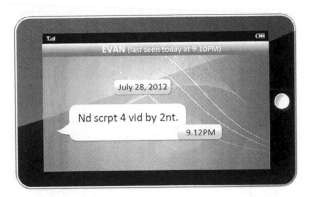

The WhatsApp message says it all.

Never mind that it was after 9.00pm on a Saturday, and that the message recipient was a mother of two who really coveted her weekends. A colleague of Evan's, though she was not on his project team, she had no prior knowledge of her role in this project.

The text message was typically short – in length, detail, deadline and presentation. Given the circumstances, it was also short on courtesy and consideration.

But Evan is a Gen Yer, and this single generational reference explains a lot.

Evan was working on an online publicity video for a client. In a private arrangement, without the buy-in from the project team, he had promised to deliver it "first thing Monday morning". He had worked through Friday night, and was prepared to do the same on Saturday and Sunday. It helped that like any modern design services firm, his workplace has a sofa bed and shower facilities.

That Saturday, having satisfied himself that the video was working according to plan, Evan's next steps were to get the video script written, synchronised with the video and uploaded.

At 9.12pm on a weekend, he had yet to brief the scriptwriter, but there was no doubt in his mind that she would send him the script that night, in time to get the complete video out to the client "first thing Monday morning".

## Scenario 2

Twenty-seven year old Angel was hired as a branding and communications executive. A month after she joined the company, her manager left. During the 12 months the position was left vacant, she handled all the department's activities. She had free rein in planning and implementing a big-budget branding campaign, and she successfully rolled out the accompanying public relations plan. She worked closely with the senior members of the management team during this time.

A year later, armed with a list of her accomplishments, she marched into the corporate VP's office and asked that her achievements be recognised. She received a "double" promotion – to senior manager.

Her immediate superior came in shortly after. He worked according to established procedures, and relieved her of all the work that put her in touch with the senior management or required "big" decisions. Angel's wings were severely clipped. Not only had she lost most of her autonomy and high-level responsibilities, she no longer had direct contact with the senior members of the organisation. She also had to report to a direct superior and defer to him on decisions.

Angel embarked on an online job hunt soon after. Four months later, she left to take up the position of Singapore country manager and managing director of a Europe-headquartered business consultancy firm.

The two case scenarios illustrate the character attributes of Gen Yers.

Although Evan was new to the company, his project teammates, all non-Gen Yers, already found him to be individualistic, cocky ("He talks so much!" was a common complaint) and presumptuous. This project confirmed their opinions of him.

On his own accord, he had brought forward the agreed delivery deadline by one week. Because of the new "first thing Monday morning" commitment, his more experienced teammates would not have a chance to review or revise the video before the client saw it.

Although his credentials were sound, no one knew if Evan was able to meet the client's exacting requirements as he was working alone that weekend to complete the video.

The scriptwriter was understandably furious at being asked to work on a Saturday night, at short notice, by a newbie "who has no manners," she fumed to her husband. Evan had insisted that the script must be completed "that night" or she would be "holding the whole project back".

Angel, too, had her fair share of detractors. They criticised her for being a show-off and not knowing her place, and for being overly confident in her own abilities. That she had the audacity to utter a "veiled threat" to a member of the senior management – promote her or she would walk – was unheard of in the organisation where the majority of employees were long-serving, low-key and unassuming, preferring to let their achievements speak
for themselves.

Some of Angel's colleagues also considered her ungrateful and disloyal as she left soon after her promotion.

In Evan's case, in spite of his colleagues' misgivings, the video was a hit with the client.
The client was so impressed with the creativity and quick turnaround that they signed the design services firm on a one-year retainer, and asked for Evan to head the account.

Angel is now a regular jetsetter around the region, setting up and managing numerous branch offices for the same Europe-headquartered consultancy firm.

Enough said.

## Different Strokes, Different Folks

Remember that Evan and Angel are the products of their time. It was not their intention to outshine their colleagues or do things differently. It is just in their nature to want to make a difference. For Evan, it was to deliver a great video a week ahead of time – because he knew he could. Angel, who had visibly demonstrated her abilities but was disallowed from utilising them, went to a company which appreciated her talents and gave her room to grow.

Like a typical Gen Yer, Evan had the end result in mind. It did not cross his mind that other people may not live by the same rules. He was not being rude or presumptuous when he told (not asked!) the scriptwriter to have the script ready by that night – that was part of the project workflow in order to meet the delivery deadline. He always communicates in short forms (he also uses emoticons) as it is an efficient way to get the message across. After all, Gen Yers are used to speed and immediacy.

Angel had enjoyed running the department in the absence of an immediate superior. She found her work meaningful, and she did it well. Working directly with members of the senior management pleased her as her contributions were more obvious to the people who mattered. Despite having been promoted, she saw no moral obligation to stay as she felt that she deserved the promotion. The question of loyalty had never crossed her mind.

# The Gen Y mindset

Before we start talking about Gen Ys as though they come from another planet, it's important to know how they grew up—and the impact this has had on their approach to work.

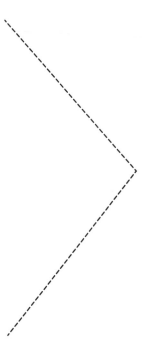

One key difference between growing up in the mid-1980s through to the 1990s and the 2000s (as opposed to previous decades), has been the way in which children have experienced self-directed play and, more importantly, risk and freedom.

Many studies and articles have discussed the increased emphasis during recent decades on the following elements of parenting and education:

- risk aversion

- positive feedback

- adult or parental supervision during play, then during school, and now at work (i.e. helicopter parenting)

Fundamentally, these parenting and educational trends have changed the way people now behave in the workplace—and this isn't Gen Ys doing. In fact, many of the complaints about how Gen Y now operates in the workplace come from the very individuals who pioneered these parenting and educational changes—ironic, huh?

However, we need to stop for a moment here and recognize that there is a big difference between parenting someone and being his or her boss. Simply raising a Gen Y individual does not prepare you for managing one in the workplace.

Parenting and managing *are* different.

Instead, older generations must recognize that some of the foundations of their management style, and the messages they have heard from their HR department, are in fact reinforcing (rather than bridging) the generational divide.

Older workers have been trained to focus on issues of fairness and uniformity in their management style. In many ways, they've been asked to provide a homogenous experience of being managed; one where everyone is treated the same way. Yet, this is a recipe for failure in the Millennial workplace.

Managers need to develop a more individual approach, one that addresses the needs and motivations of individuals, not 'employees', as if they were one homogenous group with the same thoughts and motivations. After all, one Gen Y employee won't be the same as the next, and the real answer lies in finding appropriate ways to treat people fairly, but differently.

Of course, we've had individuals in the workplace for hundreds of years… but we've not managed them that way. Oops.

In understanding the foundations of Gen Y, we cannot ignore the role of technology. While technology has influenced all of us, Gen Y has evolved with technology as a life center. It has particularly influenced their communication styles—partly because parents have been less inclined to let their children roam the outside world, and instead have allowed them to do so online, in the comfort and protection of their home.

Believe it or not, this hasn't always had disastrous outcomes. Millennials have developed a new version of community, friendship and connectivity. And, the networks they've learned to form are not always superficial, meaningless and disposable—the Arab Spring has proven this.

Prior to December 2010, we may have argued that these social networks, although global, broad, and voluminous, were essentially tenuous in nature. After the Arab Spring, it became clear that they aren't tenuous at all—they are tenacious. In fact, they are powerful.

Not to diminish broader issues, but these were the first revolutions where SIM cards trumped bullets. What would Paul Revere or Thomas Jefferson say? How would Mao have leveraged this? Would Churchill have smiled?

Gen Ys ability to build, shape, dismantle, evolve and grow networks quickly and easily is one thing. But their ability to create networks that are genuine forces for change is something else entirely. We often minimize social media as pure entertainment. It's not, and proficiency in using it is a skill that has genuine applications in the workplace.

The foundations of Gen Y are different from the previous generations. They've been parented and educated differently, and the technology that may have influenced all of us has fundamentally shaped them. Broadly speaking, Gen Ys tend to value and expect:

- Constant feedback

- Connectivity

- Self-expression

- Opportunity and reward for a job well done

FIGURE 3. Generational mindset differences

|  | BABY BOOMERS | GENERATIONS X AND Y |
|---|---|---|
| Work/Life Balance | 'Live to Work' | 'Work to Live' |
| Job Stability | Seek job stability, security | Are comfortable with job changes |
| Job Expectations | Respect Authority  Expect to have and to earn rewards | Question formal authority  Want immediate payoffs  Demand change and fun |
| Technology | Learned as adults | Technologically savvy |

This means that managers and organizations as entities have a new challenge. Instead of 'managing' Gen Ys, they need to study what makes them tick on an individual level. They need to understand them, and this is something no generation ever does easily. However, if you understand the demographics, this time it's non-negotiable.

## Connectivity is meaning

Members of Gen Y place a high value on connections. In fact, a recent Cisco report found that roughly half of students and young professionals surveyed considered access to the Internet nearly as important as water, food, air and shelter; more than half of students felt that they could not live without the Internet.

From their earliest childhood, members of Gen Y have used technology and devices to connect them with learning, knowledge, information, entertainment—and people.

Yes, we need constant feedback, that's part of who we are, and it's part of what we're used to from posting things on social media. Tools like Facebook are just so powerful. Through them, I'm exposed to the details of hundreds of people's lives every second of the day. I'm constantly seeing how they're progressing and it makes me reflect on my own life and ask myself, 'How can I be better?'

FREELANCE DIRECTOR, AUSTRALIA

Think for a moment about how you define the concept of a 'friend'. For younger generations, keeping up-to-date with social media feeds is a way to connect; it is (again according to the Cisco report) a close second to actually spending time with people. Previous generations just didn't have the luxury of connecting with people in these ways—at least not as their ideas of how the world works were forming.

It was well-educated and tech-literate Gen Xs and young Baby Boomers that infused computing technology into the innovative learning environments of young, blossoming Gen Ys. As the early 1990s passed, connection was no longer defined within the classroom or Local Area Networks (LAN) of Gen Y's inner circle. Instead, they were empowered to connect their imagination and learning environment with a global resource—the World Wide Web. This enabled Ys to interact with peers around the world on classroom projects, research studies and even extracurricular interests. And just as many Ys were entering their high school years—when they were laying the foundations of their peer-to-peer relationships—the Internet quite quickly transformed into an environment of 'user-generated content' and individual expression.

Today, connectivity is what Ys expect. They are the 'Now' generation because they can be. Instant gratification. Rising expectations for customization. Now. Now. Now. From pre-packaged foods to instant feedback on their social media posts, this generation is accustomed to a level of 'now' that previous generations just couldn't have—and it has made them more open, less concerned with privacy and often less likely to keep their opinions to themselves.

As a digitally connected generation, Gen Y has also been afforded the luxury of exploring diversity for much of their formative years. This understanding and appreciation of cultural difference and inclusion has exposed them to social issues and diverse needs. Humanitarian causes, local/community-focused needs and social awareness have been, and continue to be, defining traits of this generation. The depth and reach of connectivity they have been able to achieve has helped them create meaning in their lives—shared meaning and commonality in even the most unlikely places.

Even the most mundane activities can elicit rapid feedback. Jason is out with his friends at a local pizza place… he pulls out his iPhone and 'checks-in', posting "I like pizza!" In the time it takes he and his friends to finish dinner, settle the check, and head to cars, taxis or subways, he's already accumulated numerous 'likes'.

Instant feedback, instant validation.

Consider how different this experience is to his workplace. When does he get his performance feedback? Once a year. Once a year? "I like pizza" gets immediate feedback yet his career is reviewed only at broad intervals.

Everyone wants to give back and feel like they are doing something good. Your job should involve helping people in some way, whether directly through the work, or through outside activities. This helps give you meaning."

MARKETING SPECIALIST, USA

We need to learn from this.

The Gen Y heart is worn on its sleeve. It's there for all to see (and hopefully to 'like'). If we underestimate this 'validation/feedback gap' that exists in most workplaces for Gen Y we will have a serious slide in motivation on our hands.

## Access-all-areas

Hierarchies can be great frameworks for organizing ourselves, but Gen Ys are less inclined to 'get' them, or take them at face value. This is something corporate leaders really struggle to understand and it's no wonder—after all, what's the alternative?

Collaboration.

For as long as anyone can recall, managers and leaders have been there to check, balance and guide decision making. They have more experience, deeper knowledge and can effectively weigh up a greater number of issues and choices. Right?

Well, we all know that managers differ vastly in their ability, motivations and style. This is one of the weaknesses of hierarchical structures and Gen Ys are much less tolerant of this structural issue within organizations. They prefer intricately, although fully, connected, cross-functional ways of operating regardless of location, rank or role. They prefer dialogue and informality, which is in stark contrast to how communication is handled in many businesses.

While organizations large and small have focused their efforts on developing the kind of one-way, top-down monologue that favors platitudes over specifics and transparency, Gen Y has led the charge in communicating every topic—from the Boston bombings to Bieber—in just 140 characters. We spent so long honing a corporatized style of communication based on formality, that frankly, we can't be sure yet if Gen Y's approach is an upgrade. Vowels are dropped, contractions are taken to a new level, and there is more 'noise' than ever. However, one thing is clear: in this space, 'spin' rarely cuts through.; opinion rather than rhetoric, rules.

Gen Y has had much more experience with making productive connections across traditional boundaries, as well as participating in global discussions about wide-ranging interests, than their older counterparts. They're generally more participative, and they believe that this is what organizations want and need from them.

Some organizations have very rigid rules about whom you can speak to if you have an idea or want to fix a problem. It's frustrating when I have an idea but can't go directly to the person it's most relevant to. As I see it, it's a waste of time for the organization if my direct manager has to get involved to progress a solution. It devalues ideas; they should be taken on merit, not based on who has them.

COMMUNICATIONS ADVISOR, AUSTRALIA

They're not thinking, 'It's all about me'. They're thinking, 'I need to contribute'. And this is a critical difference. Where older generations might interpret self-centeredness in some of the ways that members of Gen Y speak and interact, it's actually more that Gen Y assumes that to be useful they must put up their hands and be heard.

The Gen Y reach is global, 24/7 and it's ready to join any conversation that seems relevant or interesting.

**FIGURE 4. Median texts per day**

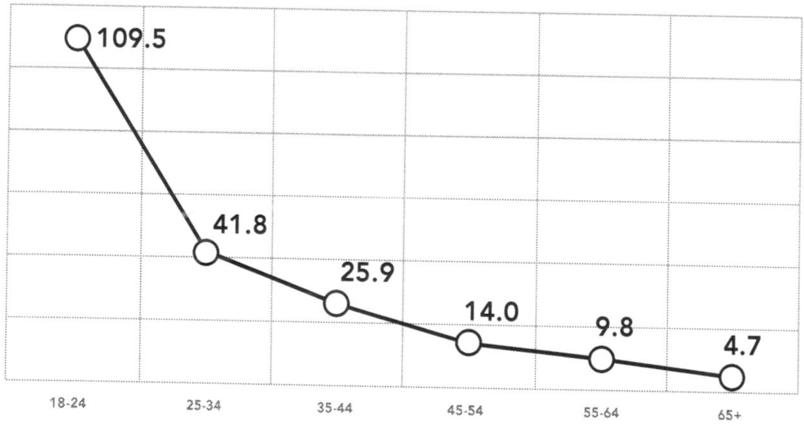

| 18-24 | 25-34 | 35-44 | 45-54 | 55-64 | 65+ |

109.5 · 41.8 · 25.9 · 14.0 · 9.8 · 4.7

## Managing meaning and reward

In recent PwC research, Millennials talked about 'compromise' in accepting jobs during the recent recession. Then they happily explained that they were looking for alternative employment. Our own research reflects this same trend—at least 50 percent of Millennials say they are 'always looking' for alternative employment, even when they are 'happy' with their current role.

So, if they're looking even when they're satisfied, what exactly are they looking for?

In a nutshell, Millennials are looking for 'meaning' in their job, and this is primarily about their ability to grow, develop and expand their skill base. In fact, four out of every 10 members of Gen Y (41 percent) say that personal growth/advancement is the main reason they choose one job over another. And, 25 percent of Gen Y members say that 'lack of opportunities for advancement' is the primary reason they would leave their current organization.

Most importantly however, more than three-quarters of Gen Y members (77 percent) feel that the ability to excel is fundamental to deriving meaning from their work (compared to 67 percent of Baby Boomers). Unfortunately, less than half of Gen Y members (47 percent) feel that they actually get this 'meaning' from their work. Clearly, something about the way we think about 'growth' and advancement in most organizations simply isn't hitting the mark for Gen Y.

The issues of growth, career paths, workplace responsibility and promotion frequently arise for Gen Y. While many of their predecessors had a laser-like focus on the career ladder, the Millennials are intently focused on what Deloitte terms the 'career lattice'—lateral movement, new opportunities, continual development and intellectual challenge rather than a simple 'climb to the top.'

Here's where life gets complicated.

This will shock many seasoned organizational leaders, but this focus on meaning requires managers to manage. It requires them to manage individuals, not just tasks. And, frankly, many of our managers haven't figured out how to do this yet. Actually, many of our managers haven't managed in years. In many instances, organizations have stopped asking them to manage and have instead asked them to just 'do'.

This evolution has created a major issue for organizations seeking to motivate the newest members of their workforce. If we're looking at a generation that is seeking meaning in their work, and we know that meaning is different for everyone, managers need to be encouraged to understand what that 'meaning' looks like for everyone on their team. This is going to put the focus back on the ways that managers do their jobs, and it's going to require HR to provide significant support to help managers develop a tailored, yet consistent, approach that actually works across all generations.

Performance indicators and work-in-progress meetings keep the focus on the tasks that people are doing, and while this is obviously important on one level, it doesn't address the issue of motivating employees to do their best work at an individual level.

Members of Gen Y are loyal to their career or professions first—organizations come second. For companies focused on just-in-time talent supply chains, this works well. So, the effective leader will take the time to understand what motivates and inspires the Gen Y employee and will use that knowledge when devising motivating and challenging work or tasks.

In addition to creating these career-building challenges, effective managers will also be mindful of the need to demonstrate to Gen Y workers that their contribution is valued.

We found that younger workers were significantly more likely to believe that they should be rewarded or recognized in some way for a job well done than their older colleagues. In fact, according to the *2013 Kelly Global Workforce Index*, just 11 percent of members of Gen Ys said 'no reward' is necessary for a job well done.

FIGURE 5. No reward is required for a job well done (% yes)

FIGURE 6. Personal growth/ advancement is the main reason to choose one job over another (% yes)

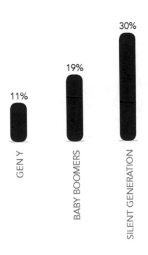

30%

19%

11%

GEN Y

BABY BOOMERS

SILENT GENERATION

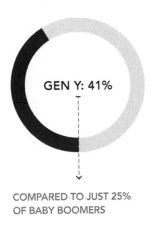

GEN Y: 41%

COMPARED TO JUST 25% OF BABY BOOMERS

But it's important to see this need for reward in context. Gen Y workers want reinforcement, not because they're impatient, needy and self-centered, but because they're looking for signposts that tell them they're on the right path, and that you approve of how they're progressing. This is a subtle, but profound, difference.

The Gen Y mindset is more about the journey than the destination. It's about what's happening right where they're already standing, rather than what might be promised further down the road. They aren't necessarily interested in a decades-long career with your company, but they are very focused on interesting and challenging work that will stretch/grow their skillset this quarter.

## Trust in the experience economy

In the experience economy, where Gen Ys live, we don't deliver goods or a service, we deliver an experience. It can be *part* of a product or service, but it has a distinct value in and of itself.

A manager is more of a consultant in a way. It is important to keep things exciting and different. We get bored easily and while there are tedious things that have to be done, it's the projects that let us use our imaginations and create our own ideas that keep us interested."

RECENT GRADUATE, USA

Just as the act of unpacking your latest i-device is an experience Apple has deliberately 'created', the experience of a workplace must also be deliberately built and delivered on a daily basis.

And a large percentage of this 'delivery' falls in the lap of the manager/supervisor.

The flow of information, the ease and quality of connections and collaboration, the facilitation of self-expression and feedback are all experiences that directly impact the way Gen Y workers feel about their workplace, and their place within it.

Getting this right for younger workers isn't always easy. It often requires challenging specific traditions and entrenched ways of operating, but it's non-negotiable if building a talent supply chain across this age group is a genuine goal.

Another aspect of the Gen Y mindset is that they are heavily informed and influenced by the opinions of those that they trust—and this increasingly includes total strangers. It's not naiveté that drives this, it's their ability and desire to connect with people based on similar interests and ways of operating.

Our research—empirical, experiential and anecdotal—suggests that Gen Y may have the most highly refined BS detectors ever. In fact, one of the Gen Y workers we spoke to said this about the way her generation interacts with the proliferation of information and messages from advertisers, employers, media and everything in between:

*We are so overwhelmed with different sources of information,*
*particularly advertising, that we tend to ignore it as much as possible.*
*Being able to get information from a variety of sources has taught us*
*to not trust the direct source, or not to only talk to one person.*
*If we hear it from multiple places, we are more likely to believe it.*

Leaders ignore this advice at their peril. Members of Gen Y are far less likely to believe what you say unless they can verify it independently via other sources. Trying to hide, ignore or gloss over negative media coverage or customer feedback about your organization's activities or products is a sure-fire recipe for disengagement and distrust. Gone are the days when the CEO could put out an internal statement (written by the PR department) about an issue in the media and expect the workforce to accept it. Organizations now need to engage in dialogue about negative media coverage or contentious internal issues—platitudes simply will not suffice.

Instead, virtual collaboration *must* become a core skillset and competency for the entire workforce, not just for managers. It must be built into the fabric of organizational decision-making because Gen Y (and Gen Z following behind) are just not going to sit down, be quiet and do as they're told—not without a good explanation upfront at the very least. Yes, this is frustrating to older generations that have learned through bitter experience to tow the line, but the genie is out of the bottle in terms of the capacity that ordinary employees and individuals now have to be heard. And it's not going back in.

Members of Gen Y make it their business to seek out people they trust and relate to—they don't always assume this will be their direct manager.

They take personal responsibility for finding information and people through their networks—and this can sometimes be misconstrued as undermining authority, or an inability to work within assumed processes. But often, that's not it at all.

Two employees of different generations simply use different skills to achieve the same ends. For example, if you ask an older person to find out how to do something, they will head straight to Google and start trawling the search results—and we all know that this can take seconds or hours. A Gen Y or Gen Z on the other hand might try Googling first, but if the result isn't right there immediately, they'll reach out to their networks instead. They will post a question to Twitter, Facebook or any other network they feel may hold the answer. They will rely more and more heavily on crowd-sourcing answers, particularly as networks become more sophisticated and intelligent in assisting with this task.

The reality is that the concepts of 'open source', of 'self-as-publisher' and of social networks as 'democratizing forces' have been developed and honed by Gen Y throughout their teen and young adult lives. As foundational aspects of how they think and behave, they're not about to leave them at the office front door each day. Besides, Gen Z has been thinking and behaving in these same ways since elementary school. In short, we ain't seen nothin' yet.

If some of you out there are already bemoaning the loss of what you may see as essential skills among Gen Ys, such as spelling for example, it's probably time to consider just which skills really are essential these days and into the future. Although those who sat through years of grammar lessons will squirm in their seats at the thought, spelling a search term correctly is no longer necessary. Search algorithms are so sophisticated they can guess what you're looking for before you finish typing, as well as show you how to spell it. And, for over a decade now, Microsoft Word has been correcting our spelling mistakes as we type. However, knowing *how* to search for complex information and instructions—as well as which tools are available to find the right answers in the shortest timeframe—well, those are essential skills. Even though Siri may be the beginning of automating this process too, for now search skills trump spelling skills whether we like it or not.

In many ways, 'thinking' and 'experiencing' are what Gen Y workers are good at. And sometimes this just makes everyone else a little bit uncomfortable. Keep in mind, if you allow them to use their strengths in this area, it just might lead to an innovative approach or experience that otherwise you might never have considered. Diversity of thought and diversity of networking is what they bring to the table.

I don't want to sit around and wait for a bunch of other stuff to happen. I'm all about taking as much or as little time as needed to get something done, and doing it well. There is no need for wasted time.

MARKETING SPECIALIST, USA

## FIVE PET PEEVES: OTHERS VS GEN YS

| COMPLAINTS BY OTHERS | GEN YERS, IN THEIR OWN DEFENCE |
|---|---|
| 1 You have no respect for established procedures and other people's time | We are result-oriented. If we can do it better and within a shorter time, we go for it (and expect you to pat us on the back when it's done). |
| 2 WhatsApp/SMS, IM and emails are not the right platforms for formal communications. The use of abbreviations/short forms is not professional. There is a time and place for digital and social media, and it's not in the office. | Abbreviations area quick and efficient. Emoticons are fun and reflect our emotions. Digital media connects us to the current happenings. It's an awesome and useful resource that's part of our lives. We use social media to keep in touch with family and friends. There's nothing wrong with this. |
| 3 You are an arrogant know-it-all and a show-off too | The Internet has empowered us with new knowledge. We know a lot, especially what works for our generation. We are confident that we can contribute to the organisation when we share ideas. We work very hard. When we do well, we should be recognised or rewarded. Give credit where credit is due. |
| 4 You have no loyalty. How can you accept the promotion and leave shortly after? | The promotion is recognition of what I have done. I deserve it. As I no longer find the work meaningful, I am being responsible when I tender my resignation. Why stay on and work half-heartedly on something I don't enjoy? That's a waste of my time and the company's time. |
| 5 You over-rate your own abilities. What makes you think you can head this project when you've never done anything like this before? | I believe in my abilities. I am committed, creative and hardworking. I have great ideas. All I need is the opportunity to demonstrate my capabilities, and this project is it. |

# Organizational responses to the Gen Y mindset

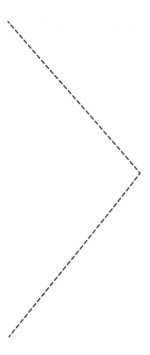

## Reinforce your corporate brand/reputation

Gen Y specifically looks for organizations that demonstrate strong market leadership and a corporate brand/reputation that resonates with them. So, it's important to critically analyze the way your brand is perceived in the market by all generations—especially by this young cohort. Have you crafted messaging that resonates with them? Or is your employer brand a one-size-fits all approach?

In the *2013 Kelly Global Workforce Index*, corporate brand/reputation was second only to location when evaluating a potential new employer or job.

Reputations are hard to change. That's why it's important to protect your brand in the marketplace—and this, of course, includes how potential candidates see you. Strong Gen Y candidates are seeking companies with a positive image, and that means:

- Being transparent and open to customer feedback

- Acting and embracing the customer view, and

- Allowing staff a deep connection with the strategy, and letting them make change happen *for themselves.*

### Improve feedback mechanisms

Think about different, ongoing forms of performance feedback: Performance discussions and review processes are notoriously difficult to get right. One-size-fits-all approaches are losing favor, and while the process must be fair, it must also be flexible enough to allow the individual to be understood, provided with the right feedback, and enabled to excel. Gen Y favors immediate and ongoing input in a smaller/shorter and more casual format so they know how they're progressing day-to-day and minute-to-minute, not year-to-year. Performance management is an on-going process, not an event.

### Promote connectivity

Gen Y doesn't just approve of social media use at work, they often see it *as work.* It is the new form of relationship building and networking, and companies must learn to use it to their advantage. Find ways to use social media principles and tools for work purposes to fulfill the Gen Y need for consistent, ongoing input and dialogue with co-workers—regardless of rank or location. Crowd-sourcing answers to questions can now yield faster results than Googling a topic—and this is a skill that companies MUST exploit. Allowing younger workers to use these techniques to increase productivity is part of the solution, not the problem.

Use social media tools built for the workplace: There are many ways to harness the power of social media for the workplace. At Kelly Services, we've used 'Salesforce Chatter', which has proved successful and allowed people to connect across geographic boundaries, as well as across organizational silos.

Evaluate the experience of working at your organization: This doesn't always mean adding services within the building such as dry cleaners and bowling alleys, but it might. As long as the experience reflects your brand and has clear links back to productivity, engagement and talent retention, nothing is a dumb idea. Ask your Gen Y employees what changes they would like to see in their workplace. Chances are, if they are involved with the ideation, it will stick and make a difference. When in doubt, ask.

Find ways to promote positive dialogue about generational issues: Where you sit in an organizational hierarchy often dictates where you stand. In other words, it's difficult for the generations to know and understand why they have different approaches and values unless they get to know each other. Providing specific forums where the issues of not just managing, but understanding, the needs and approaches of the generations will help to bridge the divide. Training courses may be part of the solution, but so too is finding ways to enable different generational perspectives to be discussed by the individuals themselves. In other words, get people talking!

## Communicate the big picture, reward the small wins

Every generation wants to know how its work fits with the big strategic picture. And even if not all of them expect recognition for the steps achieved along the way, each and every employee will certainly appreciate it. Remember, it's a journey. Make it worthwhile by providing signposts along the way.

HR has been saying that we must treat all employees consistently. But, line managers won't survive with blind obedience, and HR isn't supporting business with this blind assessment. Gen Y is different. And, organizations must adapt to get the most out of this difference. For decades, organizations have been focusing on standardization, and now they need to adapt to do the complete opposite.

Here's the bottom line: Managers must manage.

We all have managers who haven't managed in years. In fact, during the recession, we told them to stop managing, and simply DO. Then, HR had its Training and Development (T&D) budget cut, and we couldn't even train managers to do anything! It hurt, that much is true, but organizations need to get back to a place of enabling managers to manage so that they can enable these younger workers who will (if we don't manage them well) make management decisions for us. In fact, they'll take the power right out of managers' hands and deliver it to their networks. The Snowden case, in all its shades of gray, should be a reminder of precisely this issue. Regardless of whether he's deemed a hero or a villain, a traitor or a patriot of free speech, Snowden is becoming the Gen Y poster boy. Not just because of what he did, but because of his application of this deeply held belief that democracy is both a personal responsibility and a personal act.[9]

## Help workers excel

Gen Y workers are far more likely to derive 'meaning' from their work by their ability to excel and develop in their field, yet this sometimes has more to do with a career 'lattice' than the career 'ladder.' So, find ways to provide career-building opportunities, even if that doesn't mean an immediate promotion straight away.

## Be transparent about opportunities and change

There have been many articles written about Gen Y's FOMO tendencies—their 'Fear Of Missing Out'—and how this decreases loyalty and attentiveness to current tasks/jobs. The constant connection that Gen Ys have to other conversations, knowledge, opportunities and networks makes it possible to always know what else is going on 'out there'. And, this increases Gen Y's anxiety about, and focus on, being involved in the best possible experience available to them. Whatever other generations might think about the FOMO mentality, it's critical to recognize the risk it poses to organizations that do not openly and effectively communicate opportunities that are available, as well as significant changes that are on the organizational agenda. Trying to reduce the FOMO effect is partly about communicating openly regarding the direction of the organization so that younger workers know that their job and their company is constantly evolving too.

---

9   www.inc.com/eric-markowitz/whistleblowers-and-millennials.html

# Engaging a multi-gen workforce

Here are a few trends that you might consider embracing to support the integration of all four generations in your workplace.

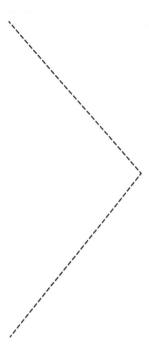

## Mentoring programs

Before you disregard this concept as 'old hat' and skip ahead to the next section, allow us to cut to the chase by saying that Gen Y have rather a different take on mentorship. In fact, most Millennials have about as much interest in being a mentee in the traditional sense as they do working 9 to 5 or wearing a suit to work. This is the modern take on an old career advancement favorite, which provides employers with the ways and means to tap into the knowledge and skills of its more experienced staff, to impart key concepts to newer or less experienced workers.

Unlike the traditional mentorship (once the domain of senior managers or corporate wunderkinds looking to advance through their organization's ranks) the mentoring program of today is a straightforward way for workers to gather the information as and when they need it. And this relationship doesn't necessarily revolve around the idea of older worker as expert. Given the Gen Y and X workers' technical savvy, there is potential for older generations of workers with outdated technological expertise to tap into the skillsets and knowledge of the younger generations.

Thanks to technology, mentorship is no longer constrained by geography and it can take place over a variety of mediums: group webinars[10], phone, instant messaging or Skype, for example. It allows an employee to have multiple mentors—aka 'a personal board of directors'[11]—and direct access to people with the experience most relevant to each mentee's unique requirements.

Offering an effective mentoring program enables employers to cost-effectively narrow the skills and knowledge gap, keep workforces engaged and informed, and demonstrate commitment to staffs development. And, by ensuring that mentors are trained appropriately (in the art of mentoring, and that resources and time are allocated for mentorship to take place in work hours),[12] businesses can reap the benefits of a well-informed, connected workforce that knows it is valued.

---

10  www.smartcompany.com.au/web-2.0/gen-ys-turn-to-mentors.html
11  www.mindflash.com/blog/2011/07/mentoring-2-0-why-gen-y-demands-a-new-approach
12  www.mindflash.com/blog/2011/07/mentoring-2-0-why-gen-y-demands-a-new-approach

Take a look at the way the Young Entrepreneur Council (YEC) does mentoring. This invite-only nonprofit organization is comprised of the world's most promising young entrepreneurs. In partnership with Citi, the YEC recently launched #StartupLab, a free virtual mentorship program that helps millions of entrepreneurs start and grow businesses via live video chats, an expert content library and email lessons.

## Intrapreneurship

A workplace that encourages innovation—where exploration, vision and risk-taking are not only supported but fostered—is a workplace that attracts the best and brightest talent. And not just of the Gen Y variety, either. Yes, Millennials are the generation least likely to be satisfied with performing the same tasks over and over again, and will seek out new opportunities faster, but this concept applies across all age-groups.

Changing business from the inside-out—that's the central aim and mission of the world's intrapreneurs. Often, intrapreneurs are the kind of high-performing and motivated employees that become frustrated by inaction and low productivity. They're the kinds of people who often end up leaving their jobs to start their own business, and it's this drive that companies are learning how to harness for themselves.

Accenture and Ashoka Changemakers recently announced the four winners of their inaugural League of Intrapreneurs awards. These awards are targeted at recognizing intrapreneurs with an eye for creating broader social benefit with new initiatives. The winners included:

- an employee of Shell, who created a program to help employees improve their innovation skills with meditation.

- the GlaxoSmithKline employee who began a project to make cheap diagnostic kits for identifying preventable illnesses, like pre-gestational diabetes and anemia, available to untrained health care workers in developing countries.

- the TNT Express employee who took on the issue of businesses operating in the slums of emerging economies, which often don't have formal addresses to ship and receive items from. She helped create a system where they could use their mobile devices as a location signifier and to transfer money via the M-Pesa system.[13]

If big organizations are to attract more young workers into their midst, they must offer the chance to do big things, take some risks and achieve faster than previous generations are accustomed to. After all, we know that just "7% of Millennials list a Fortune 500 employer on their Facebook page" (From: http://www.ypulse.com/post/view/millennials-want-work-life-blending-not-balance) and it appears fewer desire to ever do so.

### Blending, not work–life balance

The delineation between work and home is disappearing. The new normal, thanks in large part to mobile technology and Internet connectivity in an increasing proportion of homes, is not work-life balance, but work-life integration. The focus is no longer on achieving a balance *between* work and life, but to blend work *with* life.

---

13  From Fast Company's Co.Exist: http://www.fastcoexist.com/1680655/the-rise-of-the-intrapreneurs

In a recent article featured in both Forbes and Harvard Business Review, a list of the 25 'best' companies for work-life blending (as rated by employees) included names such as Careerbuilder, LinkedIn, Rackspace, Novell and Bain & Company. But what exactly did these companies do?

In the case of Novell, it utilizes much of its own technology that enables collaboration with colleagues from any connected location to be fully embraced by staff. For Rackspace, it appears to be more about providing a relaxed yet professional workspace that feels less like 'work'. Employees have an on-site fitness center, and a learning program called Rackspace University. Free meals and a fast, responsive promotion policy appears to win points for LinkedIn, while half-day Fridays are popular at CareerBuilder[14].

Making it easier for employees to blend life with work is a key issue for employers looking to obtain a good balance across all generations in their workforce. After all, the data all points to the fact that Gen Y spend little waking time disconnected from the Internet and their online networks. A recent Cisco survey of college students and IT professionals showed that nine out of 10 people check their smartphones as part of their 'getting ready for work/school' ritual. Almost half check their emails and feeds during meals with friends and family, and three out of four use their smartphones in bed.[15]

Call that balance? Well, that's a matter of opinion really, isn't it?

---

14  http://www.forbes.com/sites/ronashkenas/2012/10/19/forget-work-life-balance-its-time-for-work-life-blend/
15  mashable.com/2012/12/12/martphone-obsessed-generation-y/

There are companies that have made moves to better manage the work/life balance of their employees in the face of an increasingly blurred line between work and home. For example, Volkswagen made the move in 2011 to deactivate e-mails on German staff Blackberry devices out of office hours to force greater clarity between work and play.[16] Although we could hardly call this a 'backlash', it is possible that companies will make more attempts to manage this separation of work and home on behalf of their employees.

## Addressing the gender imbalance

Attracting young women and keeping older women in the workforce continues to be a key and growing issue for employers across the industrialized world. As women now make up a greater proportion of college graduates than men, new female entrants to the workforce are often better qualified than their male counterparts. It's now incumbent upon organizations to deliver the reward that should naturally follow.

Norway recently was named number one in the list of best places in the world to be a mother, so perhaps it's fitting that it is this nation that also has the strongest legislation supporting increased representation of women on boards. Norway has mandated that at least 40 percent of the board members of listed companies are to be women. Other EU countries including Spain, Italy, Belgium and The Netherlands also have gender quotas. Although there are plenty of arguments for and against these measures, it seems unlikely that better educated women of the

16 http://www.techhive.com/article/246973/volkswagens_after_hours_blackberry_email_ban_is_a_brilliant_idea.html

younger generation will continue to accept inaction from companies themselves in addressing their own leadership and pay inequities. Those that do may also find themselves with a significant hiring advantage.

# 05

# Retaining a multi-gen workforce

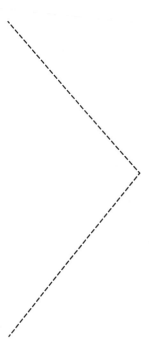

## Free agency

Throughout the last decade, a strong trend has emerged toward building more flexible, project-based workforces. This trend began long before the most recent recession, largely because modern technology has made it possible for people to connect and work together from wherever they are.

Frankly, distance is dead.

Partly because of this, one of the most important workforce trends of the past two decades has been the rise of the new breed of independent free agents – consultants, freelancers, contractors and 'micropreneurs'.

Free agents are not traditional '9 to 5' employees working for one employer. They are untethered, independent professionals or consultants, temporary or contract employees, and they move from project to project, location to location. They span all ages, professions, incomes, and educational levels, and they are interested in working for themselves. Free agents prioritize freedom and flexibility over the security of traditional employment models, and they are always keeping an eye out for more interesting or rewarding assignments that afford the best work/life balance.

Many of these are professionals who have been dislodged from salaried careers as a consequence of business restructuring and economic upheaval. They may have been laid-off from well paid full-time jobs in the 1990s recession or the most recent global downturn. Instead of waiting for new opportunities to come to them, they have started up their own businesses, providing labor or services to clients on a project-by-project basis.

Free agency can take many forms, ranging from the freelancer to the entrepreneur or business owner, working as a sole operator, or working with a small staff. Whichever way it is defined, the growth in this form of employment has been remarkable.

The Kelly Services Employment Trends Survey undertaken in early 2011 shows that the percentage of the U.S. population that describes themselves as free agents has virtually doubled from 26 percent in 2008 to 44 percent in 2011. Meanwhile, the proportion which is directly employed has fallen from 74 percent to 56 percent over the same period.

We recognize the global financial crisis and the ensuing recession would be logical triggers for many people. Suddenly made unemployed, workers have had to redefine themselves as free agents. And, we fully expect that a year or two out, the 44 percent number will fall as the economy re-absorbs many of these free agents.

That said, we also anticipate, based on both empirical and anecdotal research, that this recession will merely be a spike against a longer trend of growth in free agency.

**FIGURE 7. Growth of free agents in U.S. population**

Source: Kelly® Employment Trends Survey, 2011

What is also clear is that the rise of this form of employment has been directly related to global economic conditions. When downturns hit the economy, many of those who are laid off or who have been adversely impacted have little choice but to let their entrepreneurial instincts kick in and embark of some form of self-employment.

## FIGURE 8. Primary reasons for working as a free agent

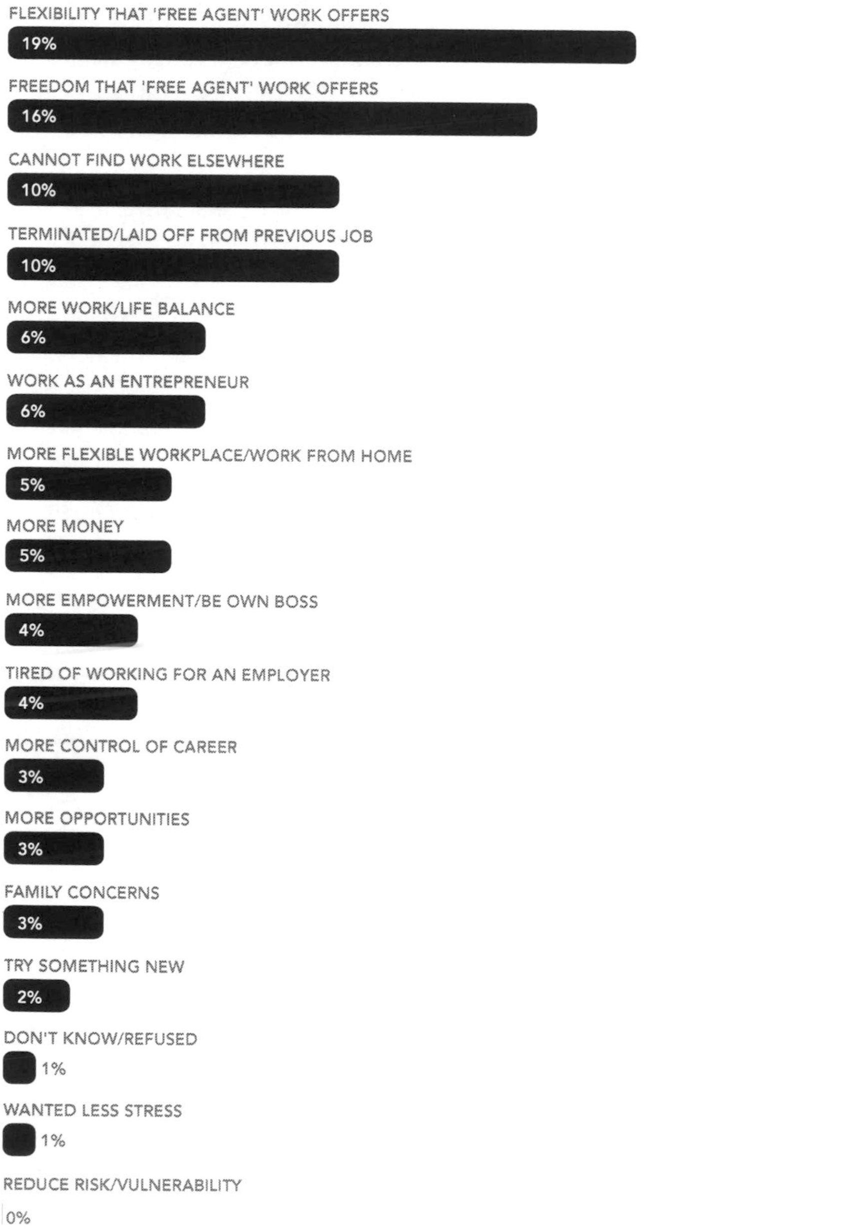

FLEXIBILITY THAT 'FREE AGENT' WORK OFFERS
19%

FREEDOM THAT 'FREE AGENT' WORK OFFERS
16%

CANNOT FIND WORK ELSEWHERE
10%

TERMINATED/LAID OFF FROM PREVIOUS JOB
10%

MORE WORK/LIFE BALANCE
6%

WORK AS AN ENTREPRENEUR
6%

MORE FLEXIBLE WORKPLACE/WORK FROM HOME
5%

MORE MONEY
5%

MORE EMPOWERMENT/BE OWN BOSS
4%

TIRED OF WORKING FOR AN EMPLOYER
4%

MORE CONTROL OF CAREER
3%

MORE OPPORTUNITIES
3%

FAMILY CONCERNS
3%

TRY SOMETHING NEW
2%

DON'T KNOW/REFUSED
1%

WANTED LESS STRESS
1%

REDUCE RISK/VULNERABILITY
0%

Source: Kelly® Employment Trends Survey, 2011

The percentage of those who became free agents because of "not being able to find work elsewhere" doubled from 5 percent in 2008 to 10 percent in 2011. The number that chose free agency because they were terminated or laid off increased over the same period (3 percent in 2008 to 10 percent in 2011).

Yet the main factors that drive the growth of free agency are not solely economic and have much to do with a desire to enjoy a degree of freedom and flexibility not afforded in a traditional employment relationship.

The reasons that people give for being free agents reveal much about the collective thinking that is evident across the workforce as a whole. It reflects a desire to be in command of one's 'self', to be able to participate in meaningful work, and to be rewarded in a way that reflects the effort and quality of the input.

When asked about the criteria they used to determine which projects they take on, the largest percentage of free agents said that they choose a job based on the type of work on offer and their interest in it. In effect, they choose projects that are of interest to them; presumably those that will keep them engaged; that will spur an added effort; that will produce a better quality outcome, and perhaps attract some price premium.

The rise of the free agency phenomenon has also had benefits for those enterprises that use contract or temporary labor. Free agency allows employers to react more quickly to the dynamics of business by being able to expand and contract their workforce according to changing needs. Employers can adopt a just-in-time workforce strategy to save money and streamline processes by maintaining a staff of core personnel responsible for day-to-day operations. When project needs increase or special skill sets are needed, the firm can quickly bring in contractors with the specific skill sets needed. Instead of spending time creating new staff positions and sourcing job candidates, managers can ramp up or scale down according to workflow.

## Branding and communication

Companies need to stop thinking of their brand only as their external face to the world, and start thinking of it as an employer brand. The brand as a 'business' may be very different from the brand as an 'employer'. Sure, Google® is a great search engine—it's one of the few brand names that has become a generic descriptor, like Xerox or Kleenex or Coke but they also have a brand (consistent globally, by the way) as being a great employer. In order to attract and retain top talent, it's necessary to provide an employee value proposition so candidates clearly see the value on offer.

- Strengthen the organization's recruiting and retention messaging to create a solid employer brand that appeals to all generations. Establish supporting policies and procedures that differentiate product/service and employer branding. Develop hiring strategies that attract and keep the most talented people.

- Build transparent internal and external corporate communication programs. The Internet has commoditized information, and as they say, "information is power." Today's technology allows younger generations much easier access to the truth, so employers should give it to them ahead of time to encourage loyalty and increase employee engagement. Websites like Vault.com and Glassdoor.com provide transparency that was not available even ten years ago.

- Create programs that entice the Gen Y community, and integrate other generations in the implementation of those programs. Traditional mentoring and reverse mentoring programs are excellent ways to take advantage of having different generations working together.

- Design and use tools that connect with target candidates in their own voice—but you must know what that is! Key messages, tone, and imagery used in employee communications should be appropriate for the generation they are targeted toward. Millennials in particular are interested in knowing why they should come and work for you.

- Consider designating someone to be a Chief Reputation Officer to protect your employer brand. The reputation of your company doesn't depend only on how much people like your products and services—your reputation as an employer can affect your reputation as a company.

# Managing generational diversity

The task of managing the generational mix in the workplace for maximum efficiency is one of the most challenging facing managers and business owners today.

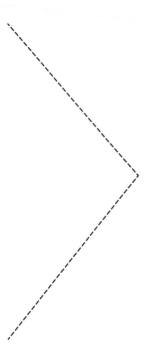

The mix of different generations and their associated aspirations, together with the rise of a more entrepreneurial class of free agents is re-shaping the way that businesses operate, and the way employees are engaged and deployed.

In trying to unravel the complexity around this new era in human capital, Kelly Services has, since 2008, been surveying a large sample of individuals from around the globe to gain insights into their thinking about work and career. The *Kelly Global Workforce Index* (KGWI) seeks the views of respondents in at least 30 countries, comprising Gen Y, Gen X and Baby Boomers.

(Note: *we do include the Silent Generation in our survey outreach, and the responses have been in reasonable proportion to the number of Silent Gens still in the workforce, but clearly, this is now a very small proportion. Regrettably, this means that those responses, especially on a country-by-country basis, haven't been statistically sufficient for our use here. We reference the responses here and there, especially from our a necdotal work, but are unable to attach firm statistical reliability.*)

The findings provide a valuable snapshot of just how the different generations in the workforce view some of the key issues that affect work and employment – issues such as training, skills, job mobility, ethics, technology, environmental sustainability, remuneration, globalization, and the role of social media in finding work.

Across each of the surveys, there is a picture emerging of a workforce that is more dynamic, flexible, and seeking greater engagement with work and wanting to reach new levels of skill. The shape of the labor market is being driven by a more global approach to work; where individuals are willing to move for the right job, and where certain jobs can be performed in many different parts of the world.

At the same time, technology advances (and expected acceleration) have given us, as employers, new choices: Move the worker? Move the work? In demographic pockets where we've seen reluctance to relocate, companies can no longer afford to blindly refuse to consider remote work... especially when knowledge workers are concerned.

There is also a new focus on training and skills development, as the pathway to expertise that will enable individuals to withstand career turbulence and economic uncertainty. Even on a more intangible level, there is evidence about the 'value' of work that goes beyond the direct financial rewards and touches on the dignity and identity that people derive from their jobs.

The explosion of social networking has opened up a whole new area for individuals to seek out work opportunities and discuss work, but also a platform for people to develop sophisticated online personas and to embark on their own personal marketing or 'branding'. Or, as Fast Company called it in back in 2005 *The Brand Called Me.*[17]

For each generation, there are different priorities. Younger workers in the Gen Y group naturally have longer time horizons and their careers in front of them. They have fewer financial commitments and are generally more willing to assume some element of risk with jobs and careers. Gen X are in the prime of their careers, generally with families and financial commitments. Baby Boomers will have a different set of priorities and timescale, developed after a lifetime in the workforce and an entirely different learning experience.

One of the enduring lessons from the academic business literature centers on the value that organizations derive from decision-making that is founded on a diversity of knowledge and opinion. Decisions that flow from a variety of inputs are, on the whole, superior to those that eventuate from just a few sources – what's commonly known as 'group think'.

The source of that diversity may vary. It may be generational, geographic, ethnic, occupational or socio-economic. In coming to complex decisions,

---

17  www.fastcompany.com/55665/fast-talk-brand-called-me

it almost always pays to have as many varied inputs as possible. One of the critical advantages in a multi-generational workforce is the incredible diversity it can provide.

Influential authors deStefano and Maznevski were writing about this issue well before Gen Y had even entered high-school. Their research kick-started the global C-suite dialogue about the critical nature of diversity and the real role of leadership on leveraging insight to make better business decisions. While their work may be 'old' in the world of business books, it's just as relevant today as it was at the turn of the millennium.

For managers, a multi-generational workforce may seem the source of much frustration, though it need not be. The challenge lies in recognizing both the similarities between the generations as well as the areas of divergence, and putting into practice measures that address each group's priorities and interests. Businesses that can manage and capitalize on the generational divide actually have an enormous source of competitive advantage at their fingertips.

The trends and attitudes displayed in the KGWI surveys are revealing (and consistent with other similar research), but what should companies do with that information? With four generations in the workplace simultaneously, managers need to understand how to deal with the dynamics of change and how to maximize performance. One of the realities of this new era in workforce planning is that a new generation of employees is moving in and assuming many of the tasks and responsibilities, including many leadership roles, previously held by the Baby Boomers.

## The workplace collision

And here we have the makings of a great (perhaps perceived) productivity collision.

From the traditional employer point of view, work hasn't changed all that much in the past five or six decades. Work is work, and that's how it will be for the foreseeable future—just as soon as younger generations get with the status quo, that is.

But the reality is, that work has changed, the workplace has changed, and so has the workforce. The progressive employer already understands this. The problem is, they are in the minority. The traditional employer, then, sees EVOLUTION.

As far as the Millennial sees it, work is in flux, just as the rest of the world is. Nothing is stable, static or long-term, nor should it be. Here's a staggering thought—the redefined workforce has redefined the workplace. And they dig it. So, Gen Y sees REVOLUTION.

| Work as the traditional employer sees it | Work as the millennial sees it |
|---|---|
| **THE OFFICE** | **THE THIRD PLACE** |
| Offices to cubicles, back to offices again | Laptops, iPads and iPhones. All information you need is on the Internet, and working is 24/7, not 9–5 |
| From suit and tie to business casual (and at some firms, back again) | Self-expression, not conformity. The person and their outcomes, not the clothing or title |
| Flexibility is required, but not ideal. It's harder to manage large volumes of people telecommuting, job sharing etc. | They chose their classes and timetables and submitted assignments online, now they choose where to work and submit work via VPNs. It's not just practical, it's more efficient |
| 'Face time' means meetings in the office | 'Face time' means Apple 'Facetime', messaging, virtual collaboration |
| The attitude of workers is changing work (not always for the better) | The changing nature of work requires a new way of working |
| Fear of loss of control | Question the effectiveness of, and need for, traditional, hierarchical control |
| Clear distinction between 'work' and 'not work' | Blurred line between 'work' and 'personal lives' |
| Social networking leads to decreased capacity and productivity | Social networking is capacity-building and leads to innovation/ better perspective |
| An inability to adapt to the current structures is due to immaturity, lack of discipline and avoidance of doing the hard yards | Adapting to current organizational structures is a waste of time because they don't make sense |

## Overcoming stereotypes

One of the most challenging aspects of managing a multi-generational workforce is overcoming the stereotypes inherent in traditional staffing strategies. Companies need to realize that the landscape has changed.

These shifts in the global workforce—demographic changes, a shortage of talent, the growing empowerment of skilled employees, and the rise of free agents—have converged into a perfect storm for recruiters and managers. The challenge for HR, then, is to develop hiring strategies that attract and keep the most talented people. Because job candidates are also consumers, organizations may want to consider capturing their attention using the same tools used in consumer marketing:

- Attract talent with a strong brand message targeted to specific people. (If you're looking for a SVP of Engineering, a Twitter push may not reach the desired audience. If you're looking for a fresh-out-of-college Marketing specialist, that ad in the Sunday paper probably won't be helpful.)

- Engage talent by offering a recruiting experience that supports the brand message. Do you understand your recruiting experience from the end-user perspective?

- Retain talent in the workplace by validating the promises of the brand message (but first, be sure you understand and have control of the brand message!).

Despite ongoing global economic instability, and large variations in employment rates, finding the right people is harder than ever. Now, we operate in a knowledge economy, where skills and expertise are valuable commodities for organizations—just as important as economic resources. This has meant that "the means of production" (as Karl Marx would describe it) now truly rests in the hands of the worker. This occurred in two distinct ways:

1. The tools workers use to access and complete work are now entirely different—it may have been a pick or shovel in 1890, but is a tablet or smartphone in the 21st century.

2. Workers now own their tools. Whereas the land-owner may have owned the picks and shovels in the past and simply handed them out to those who turned up each day, workers now often own the technology they use to access work across geographical boundaries.

For these reasons, labor used to be a simple commodity; the rich and powerful had access to as much of it as they needed, and those with the discipline, skills and ability to work, did. The transaction between employer and employee was straightforward.

But that was then.

When workers have their own tools, what employers need is talent and knowledge from them. So, employees with their own means of production (iPad or smartphone) are seen much less as commodities and far more like partners, or critical nodes on the path to success.

Because of the shifting dynamics of the economy and the workforce, companies are moving away from a focus on cost and speed to focus on the quality of each hire. They are willing to accept higher costs and slower results, as long as they get the right skills. As a result:

- Hiring managers need to be educated about the war for talent and the contributions offered by free agents. Because many companies are now using a just-in-time workforce and the job market is packed with free agents, job applicant resumes may not show large chunks of time spent with employers. Rather than being concerned by short employment lifecycles, hiring managers should evaluate the knowledge that workers have gained and the skills they have accumulated as a result of working for different employers in various positions.

- The age of the 9 to 5 workday is long gone. Companies must offer employees flexibility in work schedules and supportive structures, allowing people to build their own schedules that fit their work styles and their lifestyles. These changes are most important with Gen Y workers, who are perfectly comfortable making sideways career moves that years ago would have sounded a career death knell. Instead of climbing a corporate ladder, Gen Y workers are focused on what Deloitte has called a career (or 'corporate') lattice—lateral movement that brings new opportunities, chances for development, and intellectual challenges. Think rock climbing, not elevators. These days a resume peppered with a variety of jobs doesn't indicate an unstable employment history; it means that the candidate has had the chance to learn more skills and become more marketable, and probably more valuable. Gone are the days of a resume showing several decades of working for the same employer.

## Focus on team-building, not just building teams

Employers need to consider how each generational group interacts with other groups and with management, and focus on building teams—not just across generations, but across cultures as well.

Exploiting the different strategies, insights, and ideas provided by multi-generational project teams can help increase productivity, efficiency, and quality. To make sure employees have the motivations to do this, employers are going to need to ensure they are educated on the benefits and challenges of generational diversity.

By understanding the differences in values, work styles, and behaviors, all generations will be able to better understand the needs of the entire group. Taking proactive steps to build knowledge and empathy among all employees will keep different groups from judging others for their perspectives, desires, demands, and expectations.

## Rethink benefits

Companies also need to start building benefits programs to leverage different workforce expectations. Retirement policies may be key to retaining experienced workers who have reached retirement age but want to continue working. Investments in 'reinventing' or 'transitioning' retirees will help keep workers in the labor force longer.

Offering flexible options and performance rewards can help increase retention of Gen X workers, while training programs geared toward Gen Y workers may help to boost retention rates by keeping employees engaged.

In today's project-driven business landscape, companies need to streamline staffing strategies by developing hiring practices that enable ease of entry and exit from the organization. And this means rethinking some of the benefits we offer to staff as part of our recruitment and retention efforts. Take vesting schedules and stock options as examples. While these might be very attractive if you're planning your nest-egg or have decided to stay with a company through to your approaching retirement, it won't be for those staring down the next 30-40 years of their working life. If you're only planning to be in the job for 2.4 years (as Gen Ys are), what's the point of a defined contribution plan? These things may even be more than just irrelevant, they may well be a turn-off for younger workers.

## More Retention Strategies

Well-developed recruiting strategies that make a company attractive as an employer will help entice and recruit top talent. But hiring the right people is only half the battle—retention is equally important. To appeal to the widest pool of candidates, companies should:

- **Focus on building flexible work schedules** and the physical and technological infrastructure to support them. Start out by establishing policies about flexible work schedules that will enhance employees' work/life balance without adversely affecting their productivity. Invest in technology for mobile offices and online information sharing so flexibility can be seamlessly integrated into the work environment.

- **Encourage 'career development' conversations** with employees. Keep employees engaged by offering accelerated onboarding programs and cross-functional rotational work programs that offer lateral movement and prevent boredom. Provide opportunities for Gen Y workers to attain career goals that are self-defined, not pre-defined. Career development is now dually owned by the employee and the employer. The days when companies 'owned' career development are long gone.

- **Rethink the structure of teams** to balance hierarchy and order: Organize multi-generational project teams that will engage and empower Gen X, Gen Y, and allow mature workers to tap into the unique contributions of each group. Seize the power of diverse teams working together. This will help to achieve better results and improved working relationships.

- **Develop special projects:** aggressively manage retirement policies and programs that provide special project opportunities for each generational segment of the workforce. Remember, in a world short of talent, you can't afford to let your seasoned people waltz out the door at 67.

- **Create mentoring** and other internal development programs to encourage workers to share knowledge.

According to Dr. Nancy Ahlrichs, author of Manager of Choice, people will come to a company because of the company's reputation, but they will stay—or not stay—because of a manager. Managers should focus on developing skills in talent scouting and building relationships, trust, skills, and a solid organizational brand. In today's highly competitive global workforce, all generations are looking for innovations in the work environment that will attract them and encourage them to stay. Companies should use whatever tools they can find to connect with all candidates and interact with them in a targeted manner.

# Success stories

Companies everywhere are sitting up
and taking notice of the shift in control
that's taking place in the workforce.
With skilled employees in demand and
jobs plentiful, some employers have
taken bold and unprecedented steps
toward making their workplace more
enticing so they can attract the best
workers and retain them.

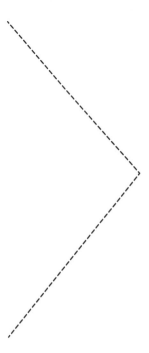

## Cisco Systems

Cisco, a leader in advanced network technologies, goes to great effort to create a workforce that maximizes collaboration, and engages employees of all generations. The company has aggressively hired Gen Ys who will soon supplant Baby Boomers as the largest generation in the company. There is an almost fanatical preoccupation with communicating to employees the company's 'big picture' vision of strategy and future development. It uses Web 2.0 technologies to increase interactions across its virtual and global workforce.

The company puts a big investment into career development by identifying each individual's strengths and allocating roles that capitalize on those strengths. Executives are encouraged to help individuals build a very clear picture of what a future career path will look like. They also recognize that lifestyle and health are important, and that a major area for disengagement is through health problems. The firm's wellness center at its headquarters in San Jose serves 18,000 employees and their dependents.

Its management structure is founded on maximizing collaboration and engagement. A complex network of cross-functional councils and boards are the primary source of decision-making. Those who are in this creative loop have a rich source of input from a multi-generational perspective, and are actively engaged, not just in performing work, but contributing to the direction and strategy of the firm.

## L'Oreal

L'Oreal, a world leader in the cosmetics industry, has won a number of international awards for best practices in managing diversity in the workforce. It places a very high emphasis on diversity in all its forms as part of its culture and its operating principles. Diversity is stressed at every level – the individual, the teams and even among its clients.

The achievement of a diverse organization is facilitated by its structure which promotes autonomy and collaboration, and has a distinct lack of hierarchy, even to the point of emphasizing oral communication over written procedures.

With more than 50,000 employees worldwide, L'Oreal has a dedicated program to encourage career development and employee engagement, built on a system of employee stimulation, training and education, and appraisal. Employees are aided in their career development by a system of promotions to encourage cross-functional learning, with geographic promotion encouraged across the enterprise.

L'Oreal takes an intense interest in the individual, with regular evaluation to determine the needs and professional aspirations of each, so that they have a defined expansion plan within the company.

## Sodexo Health Care

Sodexo Health Care needs a very considerable workforce to meets its growth plans. It is expected to hire some two million people over the next decade. To meet that target, it needs managers and staff from all generations. Juggling that workforce to achieve optimum performance is a skill that it has been developing over a number of years.

In essence, the key is in the culture. Sodexo has developed a culture of employee engagement that maximizes service quality while addressing key goals of the individual. It's also about ensuring that Sodexo's external focus is in line with what employees expect, so that there is no mismatch between what they are expected to do and what they feel is appropriate.

The Healthcare division manages food and facilities for almost 2,000 sites in the United States. Employees are engaged in acute hospital care, aged care and retirement facilities. It's vitally important that employees care about what they do.

Central to their employee engagement strategy is the CARES training program; it emphasizes Compassion, Accountability, Respect, Enthusiasm and Service. They also employ in-field training to improve performance by dealing with various elements of diversity including gender and generational differences. Employees are immersed in highly interactive sessions to help them deal with diversity issues that may arise in the workforce or on the job.

Sodexo has embraced technology to help drive the uptake of its training modules and to promote discussion and debate about critical issues. Flexible work options such as shorter working hours for older employees and job sharing have helped to transcend the generational differences and encourage retention.

Another technique has been the adoption of 'storytelling' where people from all generations talk about the way they help change people's lives. It's become a compelling way of imparting the unique culture of the organization and also a tool to build a bridge between different generations of workers.

## Best Buy

*Before we dive into Best Buy, we acknowledge that in May, 2013, both Best Buy and Yahoo! discontinued their remote working programs. Although we've only been able to observe these two changes from a distance, we never heard or read either company say that remote working was inherently bad. Quite the contrary: what we heard and read was that their respective programs might not have been managed as carefully and consistently as was needed. So, the following section about Best Buy was written to look at their early experience and results and remains relevant from that perspective.*

Global retail giant Best Buy took workforce innovation to a new level with a radical experiment designed to reshape the workplace and redefine the meaning of work itself. At its Minneapolis headquarters, the company's Results-Only Work Environment (ROWE) offered workers an extraordinary degree of work/life balance by doing away with most of the rules and restrictions that traditionally applied to corporate jobs.

Employees decided how, when, and where they did their work. They were not expected to keep regular hours or even show up at the office every morning. They could work at the office, in a spare bedroom, on the subway, or in a corner café, and they were required to put in only as much time as they needed to get their work done. Hourly employees still worked a certain number of hours to comply with federal labor regulations, but they chose when they wanted to work those hours.

Supervisors encouraged interaction between employees, and workers were not criticized for spending too much time socializing or leaving early to take their child to soccer practice. Attending meetings in person was usually optional. The only criteria managers used to evaluate employees was whether or not they met established productivity goals.

ROWE significantly impacted the company in many ways, but the most measurable impact was in the statistics. Productivity at Best Buy headquarters increased by 41 percent, and voluntary turnover in some divisions decreased by up to 90 percent.

The cost of turnover per employee today can be in excess of $100,000, so the reduction in turnover at Best Buy resulted in a stunning financial payoff for the company. The success of the initial experiment led to the company switching the headquarters campus to ROWE on a division-by-division basis in 2002. Some 60 percent of the 4,000 people at the headquarters converted to the new way of working.

For the record, your authors believe that workforce virtualization is an inevitable step for most companies, especially those with a focus on knowledge workers. That said, it's very clear that this must be well-managed and well-planned.

## Google

Google is another corporate giant famous for shaking up the traditional view of the workplace. The top-ranked search engine also continually takes the top spot in lists of best places to work, because the company regularly invests money in their employees to keep them happy and make sure they love their jobs. Fortune magazine estimated that Google spends $72 million dollars a year just on free food for their employees.

Google campuses worldwide are designed to be fun and pleasant places to work. Offices around the world offer such benefits as massages, laundry machines, gyms, organic food, bike repairs, volleyball courts, swings, table tennis, and on-site doctors. Employees have the best technology available to do their jobs, and the company encourages them to spend 20 percent of their time working on projects that contribute to their personal growth.

With its bold and innovative approach, Google hit on an idea that has been hugely successful. Creating an attractive, enticing work environment keeps people on campus engaged and innovative. Job turnover rates are dramatically low and competition is fierce among job candidates, with Google beating their own previous record by receiving 75,000 job applications in a single week back in 2011.[18]

---

18  www.bloomberg.com/news/2011-02-03/google-gets-75-000-in-one-week-topping-record-set-in-07.html

# 08

# Conclusion

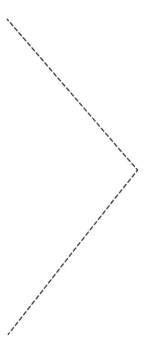

Sometimes, no matter what you do, talented employees—in whom you have invested—move on. You might have taken a textbook approach to their management—supported them in their education, mentored them, been flexible with their hours and conditions, and recognized their achievements—only to see them go to another employer who reaps the rewards sown by your organization.

Frankly, you win some, you lose some. The reality is that most leaders would rather employ talent with skills and ambition—the type that has high market value. Undeniably, this is a risk worth taking.

However, when your organization loses staff due to its endemic refusal to change tack and accept that traditional approaches no longer hold with the multi-gen workforce, then that's something else entirely.

Companies depend on innovation to be successful. And talent innovates. This we know.

We also know that the skills shortage isn't going away. With the global workforce aging and declining, and our ability to convert people into talent stagnating, it is the right time for companies to develop strategies for recruiting and retaining top talent from all generations. For workforce planning to be effective, HR managers need to sharpen their skills in interpreting and using workforce science to track trends and assess global insights. Knowing what attracts and keeps employees in their jobs is key to ensuring employee growth and satisfaction while supporting corporate goals and containing costs.

The colliding trends in the workforce are not going to change, and the challenges they present aren't going away. Companies need to act to create a talent management strategy that conquers those challenges. By measuring, developing, and nurturing its human capital, an organization can ensure that its most valuable asset is used effectively and efficiently.

Instead of managing Gen Y workers, managers and organizations need to deeply study what makes them tick—something they've been resisting for far too long already. Or, as we stated in an earlier paper, *Don't Manage Me, #understandme.*[19]

Rather than hoping Gen Y workers are simply going to grow up and realize their older colleagues were right all along, leaders need to understand that the differences are here to stay. They're hard-wired

---

19 http://www.kellyocg.com/Knowledge/White_Papers/Don't_Manage_Me,__understandme/

and fundamental to the way members of Gen Y live and work—and understanding them is now non-negotiable (if you understand global workforce demographics).

Members of Gen Y value connection and rely on networks. They seek dialogue and input regardless of location, rank or role. They search for meaning and the ability to excel—and they want to be rewarded when they're heading in the right direction. They take personal responsibility for finding the information and people they need to do their job, and this makes for a big challenge for most traditional organizations and hierarchies. It's just not how we do things...yet.

Lurking within all this misunderstanding is a huge opportunity.

Thinking and experiencing are what members of Gen Y are good at. And, if you allow them to use their strengths in these areas, it just might lead to a new, innovative approach or experience that would otherwise never have been considered. After all, innovation, creativity, collaboration and flexibility are the very characteristics that many organizations are striving to increase, right?

Diversity of thought is what Gen Y workers bring to the table, and as long as leaders learn to understand and harness its value, there is a light at the end of the tunnel for organizations experiencing the bitter divide we all know as 'the generation gap.'

The choice is yours. You can continue managing Gen Y workers, but for the leader who wants to harness their full potential, it's time to #understandgeny.

# REFERENCES

"Grow Faster Together, or Grow Slowly Apart. How Will America Work in the 21st Century?" The Aspen Institute – Domestic Strategy Group. 2003

Awases, M., Gbary, A. and Chatora, R. 2003. Migration of Health Professionals in Six Countries: A Synthesis Report. Brazzaville: World Health Organization, Regional Office for Africa.

Chambers, E., Foulon, M., Handfield-Jones, H, Hankin, S., and Michaels, E. "The War for Talent." The McKinsey Quarterly, August 1998.

The Cisco Connected World Technology Report, September 2011

The Conference Board, CEO Challenge Executive Summary, 2012, 2013

Demographic and Social Trends Issue Paper: "Europe's Changing Demography Constraints and Bottlenecks." June 1999

Holleran, Michael J. "The Talent War: Attracting and Retaining Generation Y Leaders in Professional Services." Society for Marketing Professional Services, August 2008.

http://www.deloitte.com/assets/Dcom-Global/Local%20Assets/Documents/About/Millennial_Innovation_Survey.pdf

http://www.pwc.com/en_M1/m1/services/consulting/documents/millennials-at-work.pdf

JWT: Fear of Missing Out (FOMO), March 2012

Kelly US Free Agent Survey 2008, 2011

Kelly Global Workforce Index, 2011, 2012, 2013

Kelly Temporary Analysis Reports, 2010–2013

Kiger, P. "Throwing Out the Rules of Work." Workforce Management. http://www.workforce.com/section/hr-management/feature/throwing-out-rules-work/index.html

Lam Peng Er, "Declining Fertility Rates in Japan: An Ageing Crisis Ahead." EAI Background Brief No. 433. http://www.eai.nus.edu.sg/BB433.pdf

"Living Happily Ever After: The Economic Implications of Aging Societies." Watson Wyatt Worldwide & World Economic Forum.

Lopatto, E. "Babies Are In: Fertility Rates Increasing in Developed Nations." Bloomberg Businessweek, August 5, 2009. http://www.bloomberg.com/apps/news?pid=newsarchive&sid=ac7nDxl6G8U4

Madland, D, and Kazzi, N. "Mixed News for Older Workers." Center for American Progress. September 4, 2009. http://www.americanprogress.org/issues/2009/09/older_worker.html

"Not a Lost Generation, but a 'Disappointed' One: The Job Market's Impact on Millennials." The Wharton School of the University of Pennsylvania, Knowledge@Wharton, October 27, 2010. http://knowledge.wharton.upenn.edu/article.cfm?articleid=2619

"Millennials at Work: reshaping the workplace." PWC. 2011

Richards, LJ. "Talent Tsunami: The Seven Waves of Change." Kelly Outsourcing and Consulting Group. 2011

Richards, LJ. "Talentomics: The Next Next Business Crisis." 2013

Richards, LJ and Morga, J. "Don't Manage Me, #understandme." 2012

Richards, LJ and Morga, J. "The Leadership Deficit." 2011

"Smashing the Clock." Bloomberg Businessweek, December 11, 2006. (Best Buy's ROWE) http://www.businessweek.com/magazine/content/06_50/b4013001.htm

Staffing Industry Analysts, 2010

Tapscott, D., and Williams, A. "Innovating the 21st-Century University: It's Time!" EDUCAUSE Review, Volume 45, Number 1, January/February 2010.

United States Bureau of Labor Statistics: Overview of the 2008-18 Projections

World Population Prospects: The 2006 Revision. United Nations Department of Economic and Social Affairs, Population Division, 2007. http://www.un.org/esa/population/publications/wpp2006/WPP2006_Highlights_rev.pdf

Generational definitions supplied by Wikipedia.org; MRI Data; American Demographics Magazine

## Source Materials (Gen Y)

1.  "Gen Y Speaks Out About Performance Reviews." Colette Martin http://www.forbes.com/sites/work-in-progress/2011/07/15/gen-y-speaks-out-on-performance-reviews/

2.  "The Kelly Global Workforce Index." 2011, 2012 and 2013

3.  Mitchell C., Ray RL, Ph.D. and van Ark, B. "The Conference Board CEO Challenge® 2012: Risky Business—Focusing on Innovation and Talent in a Volatile World." March 2012

4.  The Cisco Connected World Technology Report, September 2011 and 2012

5.  "Fear of Missing Out (FOMO)." JWT, March 2012 Update

6.  "Millennials at Work: reshaping the workplace." PwC, 2011

7.  Van Vuyst, P. and Van de Bergh, J. "Generation Y Around The World." Insites Consulting

8.  Palley, W. "Gen Z Digital in their DNA." JWT. April 2012

Made in the USA
San Bernardino, CA
17 June 2015